LE CORDON BLEU
HOME CÓLLECTION
REGIONAL FRENCH

MURDOCH BOOKS®
Sydney • London • Vancouver • New York

contents

recipe ratings ✹ *easy* ✹✹ *a little more care needed* ✹✹✹ *more care needed*

Bouillabaisse

Fishermen in Marseille made this fragrant soup using fish that were difficult to sell. These were tossed into a simmering pot, hence the name Bouillabaisse, from 'bouillir' (to boil) and 'abaisser' (to reduce). You can use any combination of the fish below in the soup, and increase the amount of one fish if another is not available.

*Preparation time **1 hour***
*Total cooking time **1 hour 10 minutes***
Serves 4–6

I John Dory, filleted and bones reserved
2 sole, filleted and bones reserved
500 g (1 lb) monkfish or ling, filleted and bones reserved
I small sea bream, filleted and bones reserved
500 g (1 lb) conger eel, sliced
2 cloves garlic, finely chopped
pinch of saffron threads
I carrot, fennel bulb and leek, white part only, cut into julienne strips (see Chef's tip)
24 thin slices French baguette
3 cloves garlic, cut in half
chopped fresh basil, to garnish

SOUP
I small leek, onion and fennel bulb, sliced thinly
I celery stick, sliced thinly
2 cloves garlic
2 tablespoons tomato paste
500 ml (16 fl oz) white wine
pinch of saffron threads
2 sprigs of fresh thyme
I bay leaf
4 sprigs of fresh parsley

ROUILLE SAUCE
I egg yolk
I tablespoon tomato paste
3 cloves garlic, crushed into a paste
pinch of saffron threads
250 ml (8 fl oz) olive oil
I baked potato, about 200 g (6½ oz)

1   Season the fish fillets and eel and toss with 3 tablespoons of olive oil, the chopped garlic, saffron, carrot, fennel and leek. Cover and refrigerate.

2   To make the soup, heat 3 tablespoons of olive oil in a large stockpot over high heat, add the reserved fish bones and cook for about 3 minutes. Stir in the leek, onion, fennel, celery and garlic and cook for 2 minutes. Then mix in the tomato paste and cook for a further 2 minutes. Pour in the wine and simmer for 5 minutes. Finally, add 1 litre water, the saffron, thyme, bay leaf and parsley and simmer for 20 minutes. Strain through a sieve, pressing with a ladle to extract as much juice as possible, and then discard the solids. Place the soup in a pan and simmer for 15 minutes, or until slightly thickened, skimming to remove any foam that floats to the surface.

3   To make the rouille, whisk the egg yolk in a small bowl with the tomato paste, garlic, saffron and some salt and freshly ground black pepper. Continue to whisk while slowly pouring the oil into the mixture. Press the flesh of the baked potato through a sieve and whisk into the sauce. Set aside.

4   Lightly toast the French baguette under a preheated grill, cool, then rub both sides with the cut-sides of the half cloves of garlic to make garlic croûtes. Set aside.

5   Cut each fish fillet into six and add to a large pot with the julienne vegetables. Pour the hot soup over and simmer for 7 minutes, or until the fish is cooked. Remove the fish and vegetables and place in an earthenware or metal dish. Whisk three spoons of the rouille into the soup to thicken it a bit, then pour the soup over the fish and sprinkle with the basil. Serve with the garlic croûtes and the remaining rouille.

Chef's tip Julienne strips are strips of vegetables, the size and shape of matchsticks.

Salade niçoise

Salade niçoise is a typical southern dish from Nice, usually containing tomatoes, tuna and black olives. Originally this salad did not include cooked vegetables, but as it began to appear on menus around France, local chefs made their own adaptations, including the addition of potatoes.

*Preparation time **40 minutes + 20 minutes cooling***
*Total cooking time **1 hour 20 minutes***
Serves 4

200 ml (6¹/2 fl oz) olive oil
1 bay leaf
4 sprigs of fresh thyme
1 piece of fresh tuna, about 400 g (12³/4 oz), skin removed
300 g (10 oz) waxy or salad potatoes
240 g (7¹/2 oz) green beans
50 ml (1³/4 fl oz) white wine vinegar
1 green capsicum (pepper), cut into julienne strips (see Chef's tip)
1 red capsicum (pepper), cut into julienne strips
2 red onions, thinly sliced
1 bibb or butter lettuce
4 tomatoes, cut into quarters
4 hard-boiled eggs, shelled and quartered
50 g (1³/4 oz) can anchovies, drained
30 black olives

1 Preheat the oven to slow 150°C (300°F/Gas 2). In a small pan, place the oil, bay leaf, thyme and tuna. Warm over low heat for 5 minutes, then place in the oven for 30 minutes, or until the tuna feels firm to the touch. Leave to cool for 20 minutes in the oil, remove the tuna and place on a rack to drain. Strain the oil and set aside.

2 Put the unpeeled potatoes in cold, salted water. Bring to the boil and cook for 30–35 minutes, or until the tip of a knife easily pierces them. Remove from the water and leave to cool. Peel, then slice into thick rounds.

3 Trim the beans and cook in boiling salted water for 8 minutes, or until tender. Refresh in cold water and drain.

4 To make the vinaigrette, whisk the vinegar and some salt together, then gradually whisk in the reserved oil.

5 Toss the potatoes, green beans, capsicums and onion with a little vinaigrette and season to taste with salt and black pepper. Break the tuna into bite-size pieces and mix with some of the vinaigrette. Arrange a few leaves of lettuce on each plate. In the centre, place a mound of the potatoes. Top with the green beans, capsicums and onion and finish with the tuna. Alternate the tomato and egg quarters around the edge and finish with the anchovies and olives. Serve the remaining vinaigrette on the side or drizzle over the salad just before serving.

Chef's tip Julienne strips are strips of vegetables, the size and shape of matchsticks.

Moules marinière

This is a classic French way to prepare mussels, cooked simply in white wine and onions and enriched with cream.

*Preparation time **15 minutes***
*Total cooking time **10 minutes***
Serves 4

60 g (2 oz) unsalted butter
2 onions, chopped
2 kg (4 lb) mussels, cleaned (see page 63)
400 ml (12³/4 fl oz) dry white wine
1 bay leaf
1 large sprig of fresh thyme
200 ml (6¹/2 fl oz) thick (double) cream
60 g (2 oz) fresh parsley, chopped

1 In a deep pan, melt the butter, add the onion and cook over medium heat until transparent and soft, stirring continuously to prevent colouring. Stir in the mussels, wine, bay leaf and thyme and place a tight-fitting lid on the pan. Turn the heat to high and cook rapidly for 2–3 minutes, shaking the pan periodically, until all the mussels have opened. Discard any mussels that do not open.

2 Remove the mussels from the liquid and set aside. Strain the liquid through a fine sieve into a clean pan and reheat. Stir in the cream and season to taste with salt and freshly ground black pepper. Divide the mussels between four bowls and pour the liquid over them. Sprinkle with the chopped parsley.

3 Provide a finger bowl and a spare bowl for the shells. Serve with hot crusty bread to soak up the juices.

Chef's tip Mussels can be kept alive overnight by placing in the refrigerator with a heavy plate on top to keep them closed and moist .

Quiche lorraine

This open tart originated in the Lorraine region around the sixteenth century. The name quiche comes from the German word 'küchen', meaning cake. A quiche can contain many fillings, but a quiche lorraine is traditionally made with cream, eggs and smoked bacon and is considered a classic of French cuisine.

*Preparation time **30 minutes + 40 minutes refrigeration***
*Total cooking time **55 minutes***
Serves 4–6

PASTRY
200 g (6¹/2 oz) plain flour
I teaspoon salt
100 g (3¹/4 oz) unsalted butter, cut into cubes
I egg

FILLING
180 g (5³/4 oz) smoked bacon, rind removed and cut into julienne strips (see Chef's tip)
4 eggs
pinch of ground nutmeg
250 ml (8 fl oz) cream
80 g (2³/4 oz) Swiss cheese, grated

1 To make the pastry, sift together the flour and salt and using your fingertips, rub in the cubed butter until the flour is evenly coloured and sandy in texture. Make a well in the centre and add the egg and 1 tablespoon water. Mix well and form into a ball. Cover with plastic wrap and place in the refrigerator to rest for 30 minutes.

Preheat the oven to moderate 180°C (350°F/Gas 4).
2 Lightly butter a shallow loose-bottomed flan tin, 24 cm (9¹/2 inches) across the base. Roll out the pastry to a thickness of 2–3 mm (1/8 inch) and line the prepared tin, using a rolling pin to trim the pastry edges. Let the pastry rest in the refrigerator for 10 minutes. Line the pastry shell with baking paper and fill with baking beans or rice. Bake for about 25 minutes.
3 To make the filling, sauté the bacon in a little oil, drain on paper towels and set aside. Whisk three of the eggs with the nutmeg and some salt and freshly ground black pepper. Mix in the cream and strain through a sieve. Place in the refrigerator.
4 Remove the baking beans or rice and paper from the pastry shell. Beat the remaining egg and brush over the base. Place back in the oven for 7 minutes to seal the base and prevent it from absorbing too much moisture from the filling. Sprinkle the base with the bacon and cheese, then pour in the egg and cream mixture until the pastry shell is three-quarters full. Place in the oven for 20 minutes, or until the filling is set and well coloured. Serve hot.

Chef's tip Julienne strips are strips of meat or vegetables the size and shape of matchsticks.

Pike quenelles

A quenelle is a dumpling made from fish or meat, moulded into an oval shape and then poached. This recipe calls for pike, but trout or any firm white fish, such as whiting or sole, can be substituted.

Preparation time **1 hour 30 minutes + refrigeration**
Total cooking time **2 hours**
Serves 4

PIKE MOUSSE
400 g (12³/4 oz) skinned, filleted and cubed pike
2 egg whites
350 ml (11¹/4 fl oz) thick (double) cream

CRAYFISH SAUCE
3 tablespoons oil
20 crayfish
2 tablespoons finely chopped French shallots
4 tablespoons finely chopped onion
1 tablespoon finely chopped celery
2 tablespoons Cognac
2 tablespoons tomato paste
1 litre fish stock or water
bouquet garni (see page 63)

BECHAMEL SAUCE
40 g (1¹/4 oz) unsalted butter
2 tablespoons plain flour
500 ml (16 fl oz) milk
pinch of ground nutmeg

1 To make the pike mousse, place the pike in a food processor with 1/4 teaspoon salt and process in short bursts, pushing the fish down occasionally with a spatula. Add the egg whites and blend in 5 second bursts, pushing the fish down, until smooth. Do not overblend or the mixture will become rubbery. Spoon the mousse into a bowl, cover and refrigerate.

2 To make the crayfish sauce, heat the oil in a large pan, add the crayfish and cook over high heat until bright red. Remove and completely crush with a rolling pin. Return to the pan over medium heat, add the vegetables and cook for 5 minutes, then add the Cognac and cook for 2 minutes. Mix in the tomato paste and cook for 3 minutes, stirring constantly. Pour in the stock, add the bouquet garni and cook over medium heat for about 30 minutes, skimming off any foam from the surface. Strain through a sieve into a clean pan and cook for a further 30 minutes, or until reduced in volume by about two thirds. Set aside.

3 Place the bowl of pike mousse into a bowl filled with ice. Gradually add the cream in four batches, beating well after each addition. Cover and chill for 30 minutes.

4 To make the béchamel sauce, melt the butter in a pan. Stir in the flour and cook over low heat for 2 minutes, then cool completely. Bring the milk and nutmeg to the boil, slowly whisk into the cool mixture over low heat and simmer for 10 minutes, stirring occasionally. Strain the crayfish sauce into the béchamel at intervals, whisking well after each addition. Simmer for 5 minutes, then season, set aside and keep warm.

5 Preheat the oven to moderately hot 200°C (400°F/Gas 6), butter a wide, deep saucepan and sprinkle with salt and freshly ground black pepper. Form the quenelles by following the method in the Chef's techniques on page 62, then chill in the refrigerator for 20 minutes.

6 Pour boiling water over the quenelles to cover, then simmer, turning once, for 10 minutes, or until the quenelles are firm. Remove, drain well and place in a lightly buttered ovenproof dish.

7 Strain the béchamel sauce over the quenelles, then place in the oven for 10 minutes, or until the surface is golden brown.

Parisian gnocchi

Gnocchi is Italian for dumpling and they are usually made with potatoes, flour or semolina. However, in this recipe they are formed from a kind of choux pastry, which makes them beautifully light.

*Preparation time **30 minutes***
*Total cooking time **40 minutes***
Serves 4 as a first course

❋ ❋

GNOCCHI DOUGH
pinch of ground nutmeg
30 g (1 oz) unsalted butter
65 g (2¼ oz) plain flour
2 eggs, beaten
15 g (½ oz) Gruyère, grated

BECHAMEL SAUCE
15 g (½ oz) unsalted butter
2 tablespoons plain flour
250 ml (8 fl oz) milk
100 g (3¼ oz) ham, chopped
50 g (1¾ oz) Gruyère, grated

1 To make the gnocchi dough, add the nutmeg, butter, some salt and pepper and 125 ml (4 fl oz) water to a saucepan and bring to the boil. Sift in the flour and mix with a wooden spoon until a ball starts to form and pulls away from the sides of the pan. Place in a bowl, cool, then add the eggs slowly, beating well after each addition until smooth. Stir in the cheese and set aside.

2 To make the béchamel sauce, melt the butter in a saucepan over low heat and add the flour. Stir until a smooth paste forms, then cook for 3 minutes. Remove from the heat and cool. In another saucepan, bring the milk to the boil, then whisk into the cooled mixture. Bring to the boil slowly, stirring constantly to stop lumps forming. Remove from the heat, add the ham and cheese and season with salt and black pepper.

3 Preheat the oven to warm 160°C (315°F/Gas 2–3). Bring a pan of salted water to the boil and prepare a large bowl of cold water. Place the dough in a piping bag fitted with a medium-size plain round nozzle and pipe into the boiling water, cutting into 2.5 cm (1 inch) lengths with a knife. Once the gnocchi rise to the surface, cook for just 30 seconds, then remove. Place in the cold water then drain on a clean cloth.

4 Butter an ovenproof dish and sprinkle with salt and freshly ground black pepper. Pour in about a quarter of the béchamel sauce. Arrange the gnocchi in layers, coating each layer with some of the sauce, then finishing with a layer of sauce. Bake in the oven for 10 minutes, then increase the temperature to moderately hot 200°C (400°F/Gas 6) and bake the gnocchi until the top is nicely golden.

Scallops à la provençale

The bountiful Mediterranean coast influences much of the cuisine of Provence, which characteristically includes tomatoes, garlic and olive oil.

Preparation time **50 minutes**
Total cooking time **30–35 minutes**
Serves 4

2 tablespoons olive oil
1 small onion, finely chopped
600 g (1 1/4 lb) tomatoes, peeled, seeded and diced
1 tablespoon oil
50 g (1 3/4 oz) unsalted butter
20 fresh scallops, about 440 g (14 oz), shelled and cleaned (see page 63)
8 cloves garlic, finely chopped
1 tablespoon finely chopped fresh parsley
1 tablespoon fresh breadcrumbs
fresh flat-leaf parsley, to garnish

1 In a non-stick frying pan, warm the olive oil over low heat. Add the chopped onion and cook slowly, covered, for 5 minutes, or until soft and translucent. Add the tomatoes, then cook, uncovered, for 20 minutes, stirring occasionally until thick and pulpy.

2 In a non-stick frying pan, heat the oil, then add the butter over high heat. When it has melted and is sizzling, add the scallops to the pan and fry over high heat for 2 minutes on each side. Remove and drain off the excess oil on crumpled paper towels. Off the heat, add the garlic to the hot frying pan and stir. Add the parsley and breadcrumbs and mix well.

3 To serve, place a small mound of the tomato in the centre of each plate and arrange five scallops around it. Top with the garlic mixture and serve immediately, garnished with the parsley leaves.

Estouffade of beef with green and black olives

An estouffade is a type of stew where the ingredients are slowly simmered. It is usually made with beef, wine, carrots and onions. The addition of ripe olives here gives the recipe its Provençal flavour.

Preparation time 40 minutes
Total cooking time 2 hours 30 minutes
Serves 4–6

2 kg (4 lb) stewing beef, cut into cubes
2 carrots, chopped
1 large onion, chopped
2 tablespoons plain flour
2 tablespoons tomato paste
750 ml (24 fl oz) white wine
1 litre brown stock (see page 63)
3 fresh tomatoes, halved, seeded and chopped
3 cloves garlic, chopped
bouquet garni (see page 63)
200 g (6¹/₂ oz) mushrooms, thinly sliced
425 g (13¹/₂ oz) can chopped tomatoes
200 g (6¹/₂ oz) slab or sliced bacon, rind removed
and cut into batons
80 g (2³/₄ oz) green olives, pitted and chopped
80 g (2³/₄ oz) black olives, pitted and chopped
2 tablespoons chopped fresh parsley

1 Preheat the oven to moderate 180°C (350°F/Gas 4). Season the beef with salt and freshly ground black pepper. Heat a 2.5 cm (1 inch) depth of olive oil in a large flameproof casserole dish. Add the beef, in batches, brown on all sides, then remove from the pan. Add the carrot and onion and cook until lightly golden. Lower the heat, then sprinkle over the flour and cook, stirring, for 2 minutes. Stir in the tomato paste and cook for 1 minute. Pour on the wine and blend in until smooth, then stir to the boil and simmer for 3–4 minutes. Stir in the stock, fresh tomatoes, garlic and bouquet garni. Return the meat to the pan, bring just to the boil, then cover, transfer to the oven and cook for about 1 hour 45 minutes, or until the meat is tender.

2 Heat a little oil in a frying pan and fry the mushrooms over high heat for 3–4 minutes, or until dry. Season the mushrooms, remove from the oil and set aside. Clean the pan, add a few drops of olive oil, warm, then add the canned tomatoes and boil until thick and the liquid has evaporated; set aside. Place the bacon in a pan of cold water, bring to the boil, then drain, rinse with cold water and dry. Fry in a little oil until golden, drain on paper towels and set aside.

3 Once the beef is tender when pierced with a fork, remove it and strain the sauce. Discard the vegetables and bouquet garni, then return the meat and sauce to the cleaned casserole with the mushrooms, tomato, bacon and olives. Bring to the boil and check the seasoning. Serve sprinkled with the parsley.

Duck à l'orange

The rich, moist meat of a duck is perfectly complemented by the sharpness of oranges in this classic French recipe. You can prepare the orange sauce in advance, then put the dish together quickly just before serving.

*Preparation time **30 minutes***
*Total cooking time **1 hour 45 minutes***
Serves 4

4 oranges
1 lemon
30 g (1 oz) unsalted butter
180 g (5³/4 oz) caster sugar
1 tablespoon Grand Marnier, optional
500 ml (16 fl oz) duck or chicken stock
4 duck breasts, about 200 g (6¹/2 oz) each
1 teaspoon arrowroot
chopped fresh chervil, to garnish

1 Using a peeler, thinly pare the coloured outer layer of rind from two of the oranges and the lemon. Then, with a small, sharp knife, cut away the white pith and discard it. Chop the orange and lemon flesh and set aside in a small bowl. Heat the butter in a pan, add the orange and lemon rind and toss gently for 2–3 minutes over low heat. Add 80 g (2³/4 oz) of the caster sugar, increase the heat to medium and cook until the sugar has melted and just caramelised to a light golden brown. Stir in the chopped orange and lemon flesh and the Grand Marnier and cook gently until the juice from the flesh has evaporated and the pan is dry.

2 Pour in the duck or chicken stock and stir to combine. Bring to the boil, reduce the heat, cover and simmer for 1 hour. Strain through a fine sieve, discarding the rind and remnants of the fruit, then cover the sauce and set aside.

3 Thinly pare the rind from the remaining two oranges, without the white pith, into long strips. Put into a pan, cover with cold water and bring slowly to the boil. Drain the rind, refill the pan with cold water and repeat this procedure twice more to soften the rind and to remove any bitterness. With a small sharp knife, cut the rind into very thin, needlelike shreds, about 1 mm (1/16 inch) thick, and set aside. Put 100 ml (3¹/4 fl oz) water and the remaining sugar into a small pan and slowly bring to the boil, stirring to dissolve the sugar. Add the shreds of peel and cook gently for 20 minutes to 'candy' the rind. Lift the rind from the syrup using a fork and place on an overturned sieve to drain, taking care to separate the strands.

4 Heat a wide, shallow pan over medium-high heat. Season the duck breasts with salt and freshly ground black pepper, then place them in the hot pan, skin-side-down, and cook until most of their fat has melted and run out, and the skin is crisp and brown. Turn the breasts over and cook briefly for 1–2 minutes on the second side. Remove from the pan, cover and allow to rest for 5–10 minutes before serving.

5 Reheat the sauce to boiling. In a small bowl, mix the arrowroot with 1 tablespoon water, stir in a little of the hot sauce, then pour back into the pan and stir the sauce to the boil. The milky appearance of the arrowroot mixture will become clear as it comes to the boil. Check the thickness of the sauce; it should coat the back of a spoon. Add a little more arrowroot and water if necessary, or pour in a few drops of water or stock if too thick. If it is too sweet, add a little lemon juice. Season to taste with salt and pepper.

6 To serve, cut each breast into slices and fan out on a warm plate. Drizzle the sauce around the plate and garnish with a sprinkling of the candied citrus rind and some chervil.

Sole normande

This classic dish from Normandy was originally prepared by a Parisian chef in the early nineteenth century using cider rather than white wine and braising the fish in cream. Today, the dish usually includes mushrooms and seafood.

*Preparation time **1 hour***
*Total cooking time **1 hour***
Serves 4

8 sole fillets, about 1 kg (2 lb), skinned
500 ml (16 fl oz) dry white wine
2 French shallots, chopped
500 g (1 lb) mussels, cleaned (see page 63)
30 g (1 oz) unsalted butter
110 g (3³/4 oz) mushrooms, sliced
1 lemon
250 ml (8 fl oz) thick (double) cream
125 g (4 oz) small cooked prawns, shelled
1 tablespoon chopped fresh parsley, to garnish

1 Place the sole fillets, skinned-side-up, on a chopping board. Lightly season with salt and pepper and carefully roll up, starting at the wide end. Secure with a toothpick.

Cover with plastic wrap and chill until ready to use.

2 In a large pan, bring the wine and shallots to the boil and simmer for 5 minutes. Add the mussels, cover and cook for 2–3 minutes. Discard any mussels that do not open. Strain and reserve the liquid. Remove the mussels from their shells, set aside to cool and discard the shells.

3 Preheat the oven to moderately hot 200°C (400°F/Gas 6). In a large pan, melt half the butter, add the mushrooms, a little lemon juice and 60 ml (2 fl oz) water and simmer for 5 minutes. Add the cooking liquid from the mussels and cook until reduced in volume by three quarters. Add the cream and simmer for another 5 minutes, or until the mixture is thick enough to coat the back of a spoon. Season with salt and white pepper.

4 Grease an ovenproof dish with the remaining butter and place the rolled sole fillets into it. Sprinkle the prawns and the mussels around and coat with the sauce. Cover with foil and bake for 7–10 minutes, then remove the toothpicks, sprinkle with the parsley and serve.

Tourte à la provençale

A tourte is a round pie usually associated with rural cooking, and many of the French provinces have their own tourtes filled with fresh local ingredients. In this recipe, the filling is made using vegetables and herbs commonly found in the south of France.

Preparation time 40 minutes + 30 minutes standing
+ 40 minutes refrigeration
Total cooking time 1 hour 10 minutes
Serves 6

☗ ☗

4 small zucchini (courgettes), cut into 1 cm
(¹/2 inch) thick slices
230 g (7¹/4 oz) eggplant (aubergine), cut into 1 cm
(¹/2 inch) thick slices
150 ml (5 fl oz) olive oil
1 large onion, sliced
3 French shallots, chopped
2 tablespoons tomato paste
400 g (12³/4 oz) ripe tomatoes, peeled, seeded and
cut into 2 cm (³/4 inch) cubes
2 cloves garlic, crushed
small pinch of cayenne pepper
2 tablespoons torn fresh basil leaves
leaves from 2–3 sprigs of fresh rosemary
400 g (12³/4 oz) puff or shortcrust pastry
2 eggs
125 ml (4 fl oz) thick (double) cream or
cream for whipping
100 g (3¹/4 oz) Gruyère or other firm cheese, grated
pinch of ground nutmeg
1 egg, lightly beaten

1 Toss the zucchini and eggplant with a teaspoon of salt and leave in a colander for 30 minutes. Rinse to remove any residual salt, then dry on paper towels.
2 Heat one third of the oil in a wide pan over medium heat, add the onion and cook for 3 minutes. Turn the heat to high, add another third of the oil, the shallots, zucchini and eggplant and cook for 3 minutes. Stir in the tomato paste and cook, stirring, for 1–2 minutes,

then add the remaining oil, the tomato and garlic. Cover and cook for 10 minutes over low heat. Season with salt, pepper and cayenne and stir in the basil and rosemary. The vegetables should still have some 'bite' to them as they will cook again later. Set aside to cool completely.
3 Roll out two thirds of the pastry on a lightly floured surface to 4 mm (¹/4 inch) thick. Take a 20 cm (8 inch) flan ring and, using it as a guide, cut out a circle of pastry just smaller than the inside of the ring. Slide the pastry onto a lined tray and chill in the refrigerator. Brush the inside of the ring with melted butter and place on a lightly greased baking tray. Roll out the remaining third of the pastry as thinly as you can, to a 2 mm (¹/8 inch) thickness or less. Lay the rolling pin halfway across the pastry, flap half the pastry over it and gently lift into the ring. Ease it into the corners and sides using a small piece of lightly floured excess pastry. Trim along the top, leaving about 2 cm (³/4 inch) of pastry sticking up above the ring. Place in the refrigerator for 30 minutes. Preheat the oven to moderately hot 200°C (400°F/Gas 6).
4 In a bowl, beat the eggs and cream together and stir in the cheese, vegetable mixture and nutmeg. Spoon into the lined flan ring, place the pastry circle on top to make a lid and brush with the egg. Fold the overlapping pastry from the sides onto the lid and pinch to seal. Cut a small hole in the centre of the pastry and insert a rolled-up tube of foil to allow steam to escape. Refrigerate the pie for 10 minutes. Place in the oven for 15 minutes, then turn down the oven to moderate 180°C (350°F/Gas 4) and bake for 30 minutes. When cooked, the pastry should be golden and a skewer come out clean when inserted into the pie through the chimney. Cool for about 5 minutes. Turn out the tourte by placing a plate over the ring and turning the tray over so that the base is now the top—the traditional way to serve this type of tourte. Remove the ring and serve warm or cold.

Saucisson de Lyon with warm potato salad

Lyon is renowned for its hearty dishes, often featuring onions, potatoes and charcuterie. The Lyonnais sausages used in this recipe need to be carefully poached to prevent them from bursting, and can be bought or made with or without pistachios.

Preparation time **35 minutes**
Total cooking time **55 minutes**
Serves 4

COURT-BOUILLON
1 carrot, thinly sliced
2 onions, thinly sliced
2 celery sticks, thinly sliced
2 small leeks, white part only, thinly sliced
3 sprigs of fresh thyme
1 bay leaf
10 black peppercorns
1 teaspooon salt
500 ml (16 fl oz) white wine

4 large potatoes, about 800 g (1 lb 10 oz)
500 g (1 lb) Lyonnais or pure pork sausages
  (see Chef's tip)

MUSTARD DRESSING
4 tablespoons Dijon mustard
4 tablespoons finely chopped French shallots
250 ml (8 fl oz) oil
2 tablespoons chopped fresh parsley

1 To make the court-bouillon, place the carrot, onion, celery, leek, seasonings and white wine in a large pan and bring to the boil for 5 minutes over high heat.

Remove the pan from the heat and set aside to cool.

2 Place the potatoes in a large pan of salted water. Bring to the boil, then reduce the heat and simmer for 20–30 minutes, or until tender to the point of a knife. Drain, rinse lightly with cold water and peel, then slice into 5 mm (1/4 inch) thick slices. Cover and keep warm.

3 Meanwhile, place the sausages in the cooled court-bouillon. Pour in 2 litres water to completely cover the sausages, bring to a simmer and poach for 20 minutes. Do not allow to boil or the sausages will burst. Remove from the heat and set aside until just before serving.

4 To make the mustard dressing, mix the mustard and shallots in a bowl, slowly whisk in the oil until smooth and thick, then stir in the parsley. Season the warm potato slices with salt and freshly ground black pepper and mix with the dressing.

5 Transfer the warm potatoes to a large platter. Remove the sausages from the court bouillon, dry with paper towels and cut into 16 equal slices. Arrange the slices around the potato salad and serve.

Chef's tip To make the Lyonnais sausages from scratch, finely mince 450 g (141/4 oz) pork loin and 150 g (5 oz) lean veal shoulder and mix together in a bowl with 160 g (51/4 oz) pork fat (lard), salt and pepper. Add 100 g (31/4 oz) shelled and skinned pistachios and mix well. Using a large sausage funnel, fill a large sausage casing to make a 30–35 cm (12–14 inch) long sausage. Tie off the ends with kitchen string.

Marmite dieppoise

A marmite is a covered metal or earthenware pot traditionally used for making soups and stews. This fish soup comes from Dieppe on the Normandy coast, which is renowned for its excellent fishing. Dieppoise dishes often include mussels, prawns and mushrooms.

*Preparation time **1 hour***
*Total cooking time **25 minutes***
*Serves **4***

1 large French shallot, chopped
400 ml (12³/4 fl oz) white wine
2 sprigs of fresh thyme
1 bay leaf
500 g (1 lb) mussels, cleaned (see page 63)
12 large prawns, about 400 g (12³/4 oz), shelled
12 scallops, about 350 g (11¹/4 oz), shelled and cleaned (see page 63)
240 g (7¹/2 oz) monkfish or salmon, cut into 1 cm (¹/2 inch) cubes
240 g (7¹/2 oz) mushrooms, sliced
300 ml (10 fl oz) thick (double) cream
20 g (³/4 oz) fresh flat-leaf parsley, chopped

1 In a large flameproof pot with a lid, place the shallot, wine, thyme, bay leaf and mussels. Bring to the boil over high heat. Reduce the heat and simmer, covered, for about 2–3 minutes, tossing through gently once or twice. Discard any unopened mussels. Remove the mussels and set aside to cool, saving the cooking liquid.

2 Bring the cooking liquid from the mussels to a simmer and add the prawns, stir, then add the scallops. Cover and cook gently for 2–3 minutes, or until firm. Remove from the cooking liquid and set aside. Bring the cooking liquid back to a simmer and repeat with the fish, poaching for 5 minutes, or until firm. Test the fish by breaking a piece in half to see that it is cooked through. Remove the mussels from their shells and discard the shells.

3 Strain the cooking liquid through muslin or a fine sieve to remove any sand. Place in a pan and bring to the boil. Add the mushrooms and cook until all the liquid has evaporated. Stir in the cream and boil for about 5 minutes, or until it is thick enough to coat the back of a spoon, then add the mussels, prawns, scallops and fish and simmer until hot. Season with salt and black pepper and gently stir through the parsley before serving.

Entrecôte à la bordelaise

Entrecôte literally means 'between the ribs'. This marbled and therefore tender, prime-quality cut is taken from the rib area. In this recipe, the entrecôte is sautéed, though it can also be grilled, and served with a bordelaise sauce made from red wine and herbs.

*Preparation time **30 minutes***
*Total cooking time **40 minutes***
Serves 4

I French shallot, chopped
200 ml (6¹/₂ fl oz) red wine
I bay leaf
4 sprigs of fresh thyme
¹/₂ tablespoon crushed black peppercorns
400 ml (12³/₄ fl oz) brown stock
  (see page 63)
40 g (1¹/₄ oz) unsalted butter
100 g (3¹/₄ oz) beef marrow, cut into small cubes
2 tablespoons oil
4 sirloin steaks, about 240 g (7¹/₂ oz) each
I tablespoon chopped fresh parsley, to garnish

1 In a small, heavy-based saucepan, bring the shallot, red wine, bay leaf, thyme and the crushed black peppercorns to the boil. Reduce the heat to medium and simmer until reduced in volume by three quarters. Add the stock, return to the boil and simmer until reduced in volume by half. Strain through a fine sieve into a clean saucepan, place back on the heat and season to taste. Whisk in the butter and keep warm; do not allow to boil.

2 Bring a pan of water to the boil and season well with salt. Add the beef marrow and cook for 10 seconds. Immediately refresh the marrow in cold water, then drain and pat dry. Add to the sauce.

3 Heat the oil in a frying pan over high heat. Season the steaks and cook for 2 minutes on each side. Remove the steaks to individual plates or a serving dish, spoon over the hot sauce and sprinkle with the parsley.

Carbonade à la flamande

Although the word carbonade comes from the Italian 'carbonata', meaning 'with bubbles', this dish first appeared in the Flemish area of northern France, where beef and onions were cooked in beer.

Preparation time **30 minutes**
Total cooking time **2 hours 30 minutes**
Serves 4

3 tablespoons lard or oil
1 kg (2 lb) chuck steak or topside of beef, cut into eight 1 cm (^{1}/$_2$ inch) slices
4 small onions, thinly sliced
3 tablespoons plain flour
1 tablespoon tomato paste
1 litre beer (brown ale)
bouquet garni (see page 63)
3 juniper berries
1 tablespoon brown sugar
1.25 litres brown stock (see page 63)

1 Preheat the oven to moderate 180°C (350°F/Gas 4). Heat the lard or oil in a heavy-based pan and add the beef in batches. Over high heat, quickly fry to seal and brown. Remove and set aside. Lower the heat, add the onion and cook for 10 minutes, or until soft and golden.
2 Transfer the onion to a 6-litre capacity flameproof dish or pan, stir in the flour and cook over low heat for 2 minutes. Add the paste and cook for 1–2 minutes. Add the beer, bouquet garni, juniper berries and sugar and stir to the boil. Add the stock, bring back to the boil, then add the beef and simmer for 5 minutes, skimming off any foam. Season, cover and bake for 1 hour 45 minutes.
3 The beef should be tender when pierced with a fork, if not, return to the oven. Once cooked, remove the beef into a serving dish. On top of the stove, bring the sauce to the boil, skimming off any foam, and cook for 10 minutes, or until it is thick enough to coat the back of a spoon. Pour the sauce over the beef and serve.

Trout braised in Riesling wine

The Alsace region of France, which borders Germany, is well known for its preparation of the freshwater fish caught in its rivers. In this recipe, the fish is braised in Riesling, a typical Alsatian wine.

*Preparation time **35 minutes***
*Total cooking time **1 hour 10 minutes***
*Serves **4***

🕸 🕸

75 g (2¹/2 oz) unsalted butter
3 onions, thinly sliced
150 g (5 oz) mushrooms, sliced
1 tablespoon chopped fresh parsley
2 large French shallots, chopped
230 ml (7¹/4 fl oz) Riesling wine
230 ml (7¹/4 fl oz) fish stock
8 freshwater trout fillets, about 1.2 kg (2lb 6¹/2 oz),
  skinned and all bones removed
230 ml (7¹/4 fl oz) thick (double) cream
chopped fresh parsley, to garnish

1 Preheat the oven to moderate 180°C (350°F/Gas 4).
2 In a heavy-based frying pan, melt 50 g (1¹/4 oz) of the butter over low heat. Add the onion with a pinch of salt and cook, covered, for 15 minutes without colouring, or until soft and translucent. Stir in the mushrooms and 230 ml (7¹/4 fl oz) water and cook, uncovered, until almost all the liquid has evaporated. Stir through the parsley, season and set aside to cool.
3 In a medium saucepan, melt the remaining butter over low heat and cook the shallots for 3 minutes without colouring. Add the wine and increase the heat to high. Bring to the boil and cook for 5 minutes. Pour in the stock, remove from the heat and set aside to cool.
4 Butter an ovenproof baking dish (which can be put over direct heat) large enough to hold the trout fillets in a single layer. Place a fillet, skinned-side-down, onto a chopping board and sprinkle with salt and pepper. Place 1–2 spoons of the onion and mushroom mixture onto the wide (head end) part of the fillet. Fold the tail end over and place the stuffed fillet in the buttered dish. Repeat with the remaining fillets, making sure to leave a little space between each one. Pour over the cooled wine and fish stock, place the baking dish onto the stove top and bring the liquid just to the boil. Immediately cover and place in the oven for 5–8 minutes, or until the fish is opaque and feels firm to the touch. Carefully remove the fish onto a plate, cover and keep warm while finishing the sauce.
5 Strain the cooking liquid through a fine sieve into a saucepan. Place over medium heat and simmer until reduced in volume by three quarters, to about 60 ml (2 fl oz). Add the cream and simmer for 5 minutes, then season. Arrange the trout fillets on a platter or individual plates, coat with the sauce and sprinkle with the parsley just before serving.

Sauerkraut à l'alsacienne

A speciality of the Alsace region of France, the main ingredient of this dish is sauerkraut: cabbage fermented in a small cask or stoneware jar. Variations of this hearty dish can be found in Lorraine and in parts of Germany and Bavaria.

*Preparation time **25 minutes***
*Total cooking time **3 hours 15 minutes***
Serves 6

1 kg (2 lb) jar or canned sauerkraut
60 g (2 oz) goose fat or lard
1 onion, thinly sliced
1 carrot, thinly sliced
1 garlic clove, peeled
1/2 teaspoon cracked peppercorns
1/2 teaspoon juniper berries
1 clove
bouquet garni (see page 63)
1 small knuckle of ham
500 ml (16 fl oz) dry white Alsace wine
1/2 tablespoon salt
1.25 kg (2 lb 8 oz) smoked or unsmoked slab or sliced bacon, or a combination of both
12 small potatoes, peeled
1 smoked sausage (Morteau or clobassi)
6 Frankfurt or Strasbourg sausages

1 Preheat the oven to moderately hot 190°C (375°F/Gas 5). Rinse the sauerkraut well in cold water, then squeeze and comb it through with your fingers to loosen and separate.

2 Over low heat in a large flameproof casserole dish, heat the goose fat or lard and cook the onion and the carrot, covered, for 20 minutes. Tie the garlic clove, cracked peppercorns, juniper berries and clove into a small bundle using muslin or cheesecloth and add to the pot with the sauerkraut and bouquet garni. Mix everything together, then add the knuckle of ham, wine, salt and 1.5 litres water. Bring to the boil, cover and place in the oven to cook for 1 hour 30 minutes. Add the bacon and cook for another hour, or until the ham knuckle meat is tender. Add the potatoes, pushing them down under the sauerkraut, and then the smoked sausage. Cook for another 20 minutes.

3 Place the Frankfurt or Strasbourg sausages on top of the sauerkraut, then place back in the oven for another 10 minutes.

4 Remove the meat and sausages, cover and keep warm. Remove the sauerkraut with a slotted spoon, place in a large dish and discard the cooking liquid, spice bundle and bouquet garni. Slice the bacon and smoked sausage. Cut the meat off the ham knuckle and discard the bone or keep it for making a soup. Arrange the meats and potatoes on top of the sauerkraut and serve.

Boeuf bourguignon

The Burgundy region of France is famous for its fine wines and sophisticated cuisine. Dishes 'à la bourguignonne' generally include a sauce made of red wine and a garnish of small onions, mushrooms and pieces of bacon.

Preparation time **1 hour + marinating overnight**
Total cooking time **2 hours 30 minutes**
Serves 4

MARINADE
1 large carrot, cut into 1 cm (¹/₂ inch) pieces
1 onion, cut into 1 cm (¹/₂ inch) pieces
1 celery stick, cut into 1 cm (¹/₂ inch) pieces
2 cloves garlic
bouquet garni (see page 63)
3 tablespoons brandy
10 black peppercorns
1.5 litres good red wine
2 tablespoons oil

**1 kg (2 lb) chuck steak, trimmed and cut into
  4 cm (1¹/₂ inch) cubes**
1 heaped tablespoon tomato paste
2 level tablespoons plain flour
400 ml (12³/₄ fl oz) brown stock (see page 63)
32 pearl or pickling onions, peeled
1 tablespoon unsalted butter
¹/₂ tablespoon sugar
150 g (5 oz) mushrooms, cut into quarters
2 tablespoons chopped garlic
**240 g (7¹/₂ oz) slab or sliced smoked bacon, cut into
  cubes or short batons**
2 slices white bread, crusts removed and cut in triangles
2 tablespoons chopped fresh parsley

1 Place all the ingredients for the marinade in a bowl with the cubes of beef. Cover and refrigerate overnight.
2 Preheat the oven to moderately hot 200°C (400°F/Gas 6). Strain the marinade into a saucepan, remove the beef and set aside, and keep the vegetables and bouquet garni separate. Bring the marinade to the boil, skim off the foam and cook for 6–8 minutes. Strain through a fine sieve. In a large, heavy-based flameproof casserole dish, heat a little oil and butter. Pat dry the meat and brown on all sides in batches, remove and keep to one side. Add the well-drained vegetables from the marinade, lower the heat slightly and cook, stirring occasionally, until lightly browned. Return the meat to the pan with the tomato paste and stir over medium heat for 3 minutes. Sprinkle with the flour, place in the oven for 6–8 minutes, then remove and mix in the flour. Place over medium heat, add the marinade and bring to the boil, stirring continuously, then add the stock and bouquet garni. Return to the boil, cover and cook in the oven for 1 hour 30 minutes, or until the meat is tender.
3 Place the onions, butter, sugar and some salt in a pan and pour in enough water to cover. Cook over medium heat until the water has almost evaporated and swirl the pan until the onions are golden. Fry the mushrooms in a little sizzling butter until golden, then season, drain and add to the onions. Fry the garlic and bacon together in a little oil, drain and add to the onions and mushrooms.
4 Brush the bread with melted butter and bake in the oven for 3–5 minutes, or until brown.
5 Once the beef is cooked, skim off excess fat. Remove the beef to a clean flameproof casserole or serving dish, cover and keep warm. Strain the sauce and return it to the pan, discarding the vegetables and bouquet garni. Bring the sauce to the boil and simmer for 15 minutes, or until the sauce coats the back of a spoon, skimming frequently. Season, strain over the meat and simmer or return to the oven for 5 minutes. Add the onions, mushrooms and bacon. Dip a corner of each bread crouton in the sauce, then into the parsley. Sprinkle the remaining parsley over the beef and serve with the croutons on the edge of the dish or on the side.

Pork fillet with prunes

This is a simplified version of a French classic. Rather than cooking a whole roast, which can be time-consuming, medallions of pork fillet are used. This ensures quick cooking and a more tender result.

Preparation time **30 minutes**
Total cooking time **1 hour 10 minutes**
Serves **4–6**

2 pork fillets, about 600 g (1 1/4 lb) each
1 tablespoon oil
40 g (1 1/4 oz) unsalted butter
1 onion, chopped
1 carrot, chopped
1 sprig of fresh thyme
1 bay leaf
225 ml (7 1/4 fl oz) white wine
225 ml (7 1/4 fl oz) veal or brown stock (see page 63)
225 ml (7 1/4 fl oz) thick (double) cream
200 g (6 1/2 oz) dried pitted prunes

1 Trim away the fat and remove any white shiny sinew or skin from the pork fillets, keeping the trimmings (this can be done by the butcher). Cut the pork into 2.5 cm (1 inch) slices, about six pieces per fillet.
2 Heat the oil in a heavy-based frying pan, then add the butter. Season the pork slices and cook over medium heat for 3–5 minutes, or until golden brown. Remove from the pan, set aside, cover with foil and keep warm. Add the pork trimmings to the pan and cook for about 5–7 minutes, or until golden brown. Add the vegetables, thyme and bay leaf and cook for 5 minutes over low to medium heat, or until the onion is soft and transparent. Tip off any excess oil or butter. Pour in the white wine and cook until it has almost completely evaporated, leaving only about 1 tablespoon. Add the stock, reduce the heat to low and simmer for 30 minutes. Strain into a smaller pan, then add the cream and prunes. Simmer for about 15 minutes over a low heat, or until the sauce is thick enough to coat the back of a spoon. Check the seasoning.
3 Remove the foil from the pork and place in a frying pan. Pour the hot sauce over the pork and bring to a simmer for 2–3 minutes, or until heated through. Place on a serving platter and serve immediately.

Chef's tip For a more uniform and round appearance, the pork fillets can be tied with butcher's twine at regular intervals before slicing. Remove the string just before reheating with the sauce.

Cassoulet

Haricot beans are the essential ingredient in this dish from Languedoc and give the cassoulet its creaminess. Some sort of meat, depending on the region, and a gratin topping are added near the end of cooking. The word cassoulet comes from 'cassole', an earthenware pot traditionally used for cooking this dish.

Preparation time 1 hour 30 minutes + soaking overnight
Total cooking time 3 hours 30 minutes
Serves 4–6

❋ ❋ ❋

250 g (8 oz) dried haricot beans (navy beans), soaked overnight in cold water
100 g (3¹/4 oz) fresh pork rind
100 g (3¹/4 oz) slab bacon
¹/2 carrot
¹/2 onion, stuck with a clove
2 bouquet garni (see page 63)
1 clove garlic
25 g (³/4 oz) goose fat, duck fat or lard
200 g (6¹/2 oz) boneless lamb shoulder, cut into 8 pieces
200 g (6¹/2 oz) boneless pork shoulder, cut into 8 pieces
1 small onion, chopped
2 peeled, seeded and cubed tomatoes or 1 tablespoon tomato paste
1 clove garlic, crushed
300 g (10 oz) fresh garlic sausage, sliced
4 small fresh Toulouse or pork sausages
2 legs duck or goose confit or 1 cooked duck Maryland (leg quarter), about 360 g (11¹/2 oz) altogether, cut into 2 pieces
90 g (3 oz) dried breadcrumbs

1 Preheat the oven to moderate 180°C (350°F/Gas 4). Rinse the soaked beans and cover generously with fresh cold water in a large pan. Add the pork rind and slab bacon and bring to the boil. As soon as it reaches the boil, remove from the heat, strain and refresh in cold water. Cover once more with fresh water, return to the heat and add the carrot, cloved onion, 1 bouquet garni and the garlic. Simmer for about 1¹/2 hours (do not add salt, as this will interfere with the cooking of the beans and make them tough).

2 While the beans are simmering, melt the goose fat, duck fat or lard in a large flameproof casserole dish. Season the lamb shoulder and pork shoulder and brown in the casserole dish. Remove and set aside. In the same dish, cook the chopped onion until soft but not coloured. Add the tomato, crushed garlic and the second bouquet garni. Heat until bubbling, return the meat to the casserole dish, cover and place in the oven for 1 hour to 1¹/2 hours, or until the meat is tender. Remove the meat from the casserole.

3 Reduce the oven temperature to warm 160°C (315°F/Gas 2–3). Add the garlic sausage, Toulouse sausages and confit to the casserole, bring to a simmer on the stove, then cook in the oven for 20 minutes. Transfer the confit and the sausages to a bowl and keep warm and set the sauce aside. Reduce the oven temperature to slow 150°C (300°F/Gas 2).

4 When the beans are almost cooked (they should be tender with a slight resistance), drain and add the beans' cooking liquid to the reserved sauce in the casserole dish. Remove and discard the vegetables and bouquet garni. Remove the slab bacon and pork rind and, keeping each separate, cut into bite-sized pieces, then set aside to cool.

5 Warm a large, ovenproof serving dish. Cover the bottom with some of the pork rind and then cover with a layer of beans. Add the lamb shoulder, pork shoulder, sausages, confit and about 250–375 ml (8–12 fl oz) of the reserved liquid. Cover with another layer of beans and top with the pieces of bacon, the remaining pork rind and liquid. Sprinkle with breadcrumbs and drizzle with a little extra goose fat. Bake for 1 hour, or until the breadcrumbs are lightly coloured, then serve.

Rack of lamb with a herb crust

Provence is known for its sunny climate and wonderful fresh vegetables and herbs. The herb crust in this Provençal dish features aromatic thyme, found growing wild in the hills.

*Preparation time **1 hour***
*Total cooking time **1 hour 30 minutes***
Serves 4

2 x 6-chop racks of lamb (best end of neck), trimmed and cleaned and with the bones and trimmings retained (see Chef's tip)
2 tablespoons oil

LAMB JUS
1/2 onion, chopped
3 cloves garlic, coarsely chopped

HERB CRUST
120 g (4 oz) fresh breadcrumbs
5 cloves garlic, finely chopped
4 tablespoons finely chopped fresh parsley
1 tablespoon fresh thyme leaves
80 g (2³/4 oz) unsalted butter, softened

1 Preheat the oven to moderately hot 200°C (400°F/Gas 6). Score the fat on the outside of the racks in a crisscross pattern. Heat the oil in a frying pan over medium-high heat, season the lamb, place in the pan and cook quickly to seal and brown the surface. Remove from the pan and set aside. Place the bones and lean trimmings in a roasting pan and roast in the oven for 20–30 minutes, then remove to cool. Increase the oven temperature to very hot 250°C (500°F/Gas 10).

2 To make the lamb jus, remove the bones and trimmings from the roasting pan, leaving the fat behind, and place them in a pan with the onion, garlic and 400 ml (12³/4 fl oz) water. Bring to a simmer and cook for 30 minutes.

3 To make the herb crust, mix together in a large bowl the fresh breadcrumbs, chopped garlic, parsley and thyme leaves. Season and mix in the softened butter to form a paste.

4 Press a layer of the herb crust onto the fat side of the racks, leaving the bones and the bottom clean. Place the crusted racks in a roasting pan and lightly brown in the oven for 20–25 minutes. Set aside and keep warm.

5 Strain the jus into another pan and cook until reduced in volume by three quarters, skimming off the fat or impurities that float to the surface. Serve on the side in a sauce boat.

Chef's tip Ask your butcher to trim and clean the racks for you. You can also do it yourself by cutting away the fat and meat to expose the bones, then scraping the bones until perfectly clean.

Cider apple chicken with mushroom sauce

*The traditional French name for this recipe is Poulet Vallée d'Auge. The Auge Valley
is in Normandy and this recipe makes good use of local ingredients: butter, Calvados, cider,
cream and apples from the dairy farms and apple orchards.*

*Preparation time **25 minutes***
*Total cooking time **1 hour***
*Serves **4***

1 chicken, weighing 1.8 kg (3 lb 10 oz)
60 g (2 oz) unsalted butter
oil, for cooking
60 ml (2 fl oz) Calvados
2 French shallots, finely chopped
500 ml (16 fl oz) cider
150 g (5 oz) button mushrooms, sliced
250 ml (8 fl oz) thick (double) cream
200 g (6¹/2 oz) apples (Golden delicious)
50 g (1³/4 oz) clarified butter (see Chef's tip)
4 tablespoons chopped fresh parsley

1 Cut the chicken into four or eight pieces and season
with salt and freshly ground black pepper. Heat half the
butter and a little oil in a pan and sauté the chicken in
batches, skin-side-down, until lightly browned. Pour off
the excess fat, return all the chicken to the pan, add the
Calvados and light with a match to flambé (keep a
saucepan lid on one side in case of emergency). Add the
shallots and cook gently until softened but not brown.

Add the cider, cover and cook for 15 minutes, turning
the chicken after 10 minutes.

2 Meanwhile, sauté the mushrooms in the remaining
butter, covered, for 4 minutes. Add the mushrooms and
cooking juices, and the cream to the chicken and cook
for 5 minutes. Remove the chicken and keep warm.

3 Continue cooking the sauce for 10 minutes, or until
it is reduced enough to coat the back of a spoon. Adjust
the seasoning to taste. Return the chicken to the pan,
bring to the boil, reduce the heat and simmer for
2 minutes to heat the chicken through.

4 Core the unpeeled apples and cut across into thin
slices. Fry in the clarified butter until golden brown on
both sides. Garnish the chicken with the apples and
chopped parsley.

Chef's tip Clarified butter is used because it will cook at
a higher temperature without burning. You will need
90 g (3 oz) butter to yield 50 g (1³/4 oz) clarified butter.
Melt the butter gently over low heat in a small heavy-
based pan, without stirring or shaking the pan. Skim the
froth from the top, then carefully pour the clear butter
into another container, leaving the white sediment in
the base of the pan. Cover and keep in the refrigerator
for up to 4 weeks.

Pear and honey flan

This deliciously light tart of pears caramelized in honey is best served lukewarm and dusted with icing sugar. The pears could be replaced by the same quantity of another fruit.

*Preparation time **25 minutes + 25 minutes chilling***
*Total cooking time **50 minutes***

Serves 6

PASTRY
150 g (5 oz) plain flour
2 tablespoons caster sugar
75 g (2¹/2 oz) unsalted butter, chopped
1 egg, lightly beaten
1 drop vanilla extract or essence

60 g (2 oz) honey
250 g (8 oz) canned or bottled pears in syrup
2 eggs
1 teaspoon cornflour or potato starch
40 g (1¹/4 oz) sugar
125 ml (4 fl oz) cream
icing sugar, for dusting

1 To make the pastry, preheat the oven to moderately hot 200°C (400°F/Gas 6). Sift the flour into a large bowl, add the sugar and butter and rub in with your fingers until the mixture is evenly coloured and resembles fine breadcrumbs. Shake the bowl to check all the butter has been incorporated, then make a well in the centre. Pour the egg and vanilla into the well and use your hands to draw the dry ingredients into the liquid until a dough begins to form. Add a little water if necessary. Bring the dough together and shape into a rough ball. Do not overwork or the pastry will be tough. Cover with plastic wrap and leave to rest in the refrigerator for 20 minutes.

2 Place the honey in a pan, bring to the boil over medium heat and cook until it darkens in colour. Drain the pears and retain the liquid. Cut into 1 cm (¹/2 inch) cubes and roll around in the caramelized honey. In a bowl, whisk together the eggs, cornflour, sugar and cream and set aside.

3 Roll out the dough to a 3 mm (¹/8 inch) thickness and line a shallow loose-bottomed flan tin, 18–20 cm (7–8 inches) across the base. Cover with a round of baking paper and fill with either baking beans or rice. Place in the refrigerator for 5 minutes, then bake for 10 minutes. Remove the beans or rice and paper, sprinkle the bottom with the pear, reserving the honey, and cover with the egg mixture. Bake for 12 minutes, then reduce the heat to warm 170°C (325°F/Gas 3) and bake for another 25 minutes.

4 In a small saucepan, cook the honey and pear liquid until thick and syrupy and then brush over the surface of the tart. Dust with sifted icing sugar before serving.

Cherry clafoutis

A rustic dessert from the Limousin region in central France. Traditionally, a clafoutis was cooked slowly during the day while the workers were out in the fields.

*Preparation time **25 minutes***
*Total cooking time **30 minutes***
Serves 4

80 g (2³/4 oz) plain flour
2 eggs
60 g (2 oz) caster sugar
200 ml (6¹/2 fl oz) milk
50 ml (1³/4 fl oz) thick (double) cream
40 g (1¹/4 oz) unsalted butter, melted
400 g (12³/4 oz) fresh cherries, washed and pitted
icing sugar, for dusting

1 Preheat the oven to warm 160°C (315°F/Gas 2–3). Sift the flour into a mixing bowl and make a well in the centre. Add the eggs and whisk until smooth. Add the sugar, milk, cream and melted butter, mixing well after each addition. Strain in order to remove any lumps.

2 Butter a 1.5 litre ovenproof dish. Sprinkle the cherries over the bottom then pour in the batter. Bake in the oven for 30 minutes, or until an inserted knife tip comes out of the batter clean. Serve warm, generously dusted with icing sugar.

Chef's tip If fresh cherries are unavailable, they can be replaced with canned. Drain well, then pan-fry in a little butter, adding 1–2 tablespoons Kirsch. Cook until the Kirsch has evaporated.

Tarte Tatin

*This delicious 'upside down' tart was invented by the Tatin sisters, who ran
a hotel-restaurant in the Sologne region at the turn of the century. It was first served
in Paris at Maxim's, where it is still a house speciality.*

Preparation time **50 minutes + 20 minutes chilling**
Total cooking time **1 hour 20 minutes**
Serves 6–8

PASTRY
125 g (4 oz) unsalted butter, at room temperature
50 g (1³/4 oz) caster sugar
1 egg, beaten
1–2 drops vanilla extract or essence, optional
200 g (6¹/2 oz) plain flour

60 g (2 oz) sugar
90 g (3 oz) unsalted butter
*8–11 medium Pink ladies, Fuji or Cox apples, about
   220 g (7 oz) each, peeled, cored and halved and
   tossed in 1 teaspoon lemon juice*

1 To make the pastry, cream the butter and sugar in a
bowl, using a wooden spoon or electric beaters. Add the
egg and vanilla in two or three stages, mixing well before
each addition. Sift the flour with a pinch of salt, add to
the mixture and stir until smooth. Draw the dough
together with your hands to form a rough ball, flatten
with the palm of your hand to a 1 cm (1/2 inch) thickness
and wrap in plastic wrap. Chill for 20 minutes.

2 Preheat the oven to moderate 180°C (350°F/Gas 4).
Roll out the chilled dough to a circle, 3 mm (1/8 inch)
thick, place on a lined tray and refrigerate.

3 In a 20 cm (8 inch) ovenproof frying pan (with
sloping sides), place the sugar and butter together. Cook
over medium heat, stirring constantly, for 10 minutes, or
until it begins to bubble and colour slightly.

4 Cook the apples and add the pastry following the
method in the Chef's techniques on page 62. Make a
few small incisions in the pastry to allow steam to
escape, then place the pan on a tray and bake for about
15–20 minutes, or until the pastry is nicely coloured.

5 Remove from the oven and allow to sit for 2 minutes.
Place a serving platter over the pan and tilt to allow any
juices to flow out into a bowl. In one swift motion, flip
the pan over, giving it a good shake to ensure the apples
loosen. Carefully lift the pan. If there is any extra liquid,
drizzle it over the apples. Serve warm.

Chef's tips It is important to have a big enough pan to
allow you to baste the apples. You also need to be
careful of caramel catching on the bottom of the pan.

The apples will give off liquid, so the caramel must
be well reduced before the pastry goes on.

Touraine crémets with raspberry coulis

*A speciality of Angers and Saumur, these simple yet delicious crémets may be served
with a raspberry coulis or fresh berries. Traditionally they are made
without the icing sugar and served with fresh cream and plenty of white sugar.*

*Preparation time **20 minutes + 1 hour setting time***
Serves 4

200 ml (6¹/2 fl oz) cream, for whipping
300 g (10 oz) fromage frais or cream cheese (see
  Chef's tip)
50 g (1³/4 oz) icing sugar
fresh mint sprigs, to garnish
red berries, to garnish

RASPBERRY COULIS
400 g (12³/4 oz) fresh raspberries
80 g (2³/4 oz) icing sugar
few drops of lemon juice

1 Line four 9 cm (3¹/2 inch) wide ramekins with pieces
of muslin large enough to hang over the top of the
moulds. Pour the cream into a bowl, place the bowl into
a bowl filled with ice cubes and a little water and lightly
whip the cream until it leaves a trail, but just runs if the
bowl is tipped. Add the fromage frais or cream cheese
and whip until creamy. Stir in the icing sugar and pour
the mixture into the ramekin dishes. Fold the excess
muslin over to cover the mixture and place in the
refrigerator for at least 1 hour.

2 To make the raspberry coulis, blend the raspberries in
a food processor, add the sugar and lemon juice to taste
and then pass the purée through a fine sieve. To obtain
a deep red coulis, do not blend the purée for too long as
doing this incorporates air and will cause it to lose its
bright red colour and start to become pink.

3 Turn the muslin back over the top edge of the
moulds, then turn the moulds over carefully onto
individual plates and remove the moulds then the
muslin. Pour some of the raspberry coulis around each
crémet and decorate with the mint and red berries.

Chef's tip For a very light and refreshing dessert, use
fromage frais, and for a richer dessert, use cream cheese.

Rice pudding tart

The crusaders originally brought rice to France and in the seventeenth century the French first attempted its cultivation, without much success. Today, however, there is a successful rice-growing industry in the Camargue.

*Preparation time **40 minutes + 45 minutes resting***
*Total cooking time **1 hour***
*Serves **6–8***

PASTRY
250 g (8 oz) plain flour
75 g (2¹/₂ oz) unsalted butter, chilled and cut in cubes
4 tablespoons milk
12 g (¹/₂ oz) fresh yeast or 6 g (¹/₄ oz) dried yeast
¹/₂ tablespoon oil
I egg

500 ml (16 fl oz) milk
ground cinnamon, to taste
100 g (3¹/₄ oz) caster sugar
70 g (2¹/₄ oz) short-grain rice
2 egg yolks
3 egg whites
icing sugar, to dust

1 To make the pastry, preheat the oven to warm 160°C (315°F/Gas 2–3). Sift the flour into a large bowl, add the butter and rub in with a quick, light action of your fingertips until the butter is incorporated and the flour is sandy in texture. Warm the milk in a small pan, then stir in the yeast. Make a well in the centre of the flour mixture and add the milk, oil and egg. Mix until a dough forms, then knead until smooth. Place in a lightly oiled bowl, cover with a tea towel and leave in a warm place to rise for 45 minutes, or until doubled in volume.

2 In a pan, heat the milk with the cinnamon and 70 g (2¹/₄ oz) of the sugar. Add the rice and cook over low heat for 15 minutes, or until the rice is tender, stirring frequently to prevent sticking. Remove from the heat, mix in the egg yolks until well combined and set aside.

3 Punch down the dough. Place on a lightly floured surface, roll out to a circle 3 mm (¹/₈ inch) thick, and line a deep loose-bottom flan tin, 22 cm (8³/₄ inches) across the base. Trim the edges and refrigerate until ready to use.

4 Beat the egg whites until stiff, then beat in the remaining sugar until smooth and glossy, making sure that the sugar is completely dissolved into the whites. Fold into the rice mixture.

5 Fill the pastry-lined tin with the rice mixture and place in the oven. Bake for 35–40 minutes, or until a knife tip inserted into the centre comes out clean and the top is golden brown. Dust with sifted icing sugar. The tart can be served warm or cold.

Normandy tart

Well known for its apples, Normandy cuisine features this fruit in both sweet and savoury dishes. Many of the apples are used to make cider and Calvados, but the leftover apples are often used to make this simple but rich tart.

*Preparation time **1 hour + 50 minutes refrigeration***
*Total cooking time **1 hour***
Serves 6–8

PASTRY
250 g (8 oz) plain flour
150 g (5 oz) unsalted butter, chilled and cut in cubes
1 egg
50 g (1³/4 oz) caster sugar
1–2 drops vanilla extract or essence

3 medium apples
juice of 1 lemon
2 eggs
1 egg yolk
60 g (2 oz) caster sugar
1 teaspoon ground cinnamon
200 ml (6¹/2 fl oz) cream
icing sugar, to dust

1 Preheat the oven to warm 170°C (325°F/Gas 3). Butter a deep loose-bottom flan tin, 22 cm (8³/4 inches) across the base, then place in the refrigerator to set the butter.

2 To make the pastry, sift the flour into a large bowl, add the butter and rub in with a quick, light action of your fingertips until the butter is incorporated and the flour is sandy in texture. Make a well in the centre. Beat the egg with 1 tablespoon water and place in the well with the sugar, vanilla and a pinch of salt. Gradually incorporate the dry ingredients until a rough dough forms. Push the dough lightly down and forward with the palm of your hand and turn over with your fingertips until smooth. Form into a flat ball and cover with plastic wrap. Place in the refrigerator to rest for 20 minutes.

3 Peel and core the apples. Cut each apple into eight thick wedges, toss in the lemon juice and keep chilled until ready to use.

4 Lightly whisk the eggs and egg yolk with the sugar. Add the cinnamon and cream, mix well and set aside.

5 Roll the dough into a 2–3 mm (¹/8 inch) thick round. Line the flan tin with the pastry, making sure there are no air pockets and that the dough is lying directly against the tin to prevent shrinking. Chill in the refrigerator for 30 minutes.. Arrange the apple wedges on their sides over the base of the pastry, making sure that it is well filled, then pour the cream mixture over without overflowing. Bake for 45–60 minutes, or until set. Serve warm, dusted with sifted icing sugar.

Basque cake

The cream of this Basque cake can be flavoured with a herb-flavoured liqueur known as Izarra, which is based on Armagnac. Traditionally, the cake can be filled with either a pastry cream or a sour cherry preserve.

*Preparation time **30 minutes + 30 minutes refrigeration***
*Total cooking time **50 minutes***
Serves 4

❁ ❁ ❁

250 g (8 oz) unsalted butter, softened
150 g (5 oz) caster sugar
I teaspoon baking powder
finely grated rind of I lemon
400 g (12³/4 oz) plain flour
2 eggs, lightly beaten
4 tablespoons Armagnac
icing sugar, to dust
I egg, beaten

PASTRY CREAM
500 ml (16 fl oz) milk
5 egg yolks
160 g (5¹/4 oz) caster sugar
2 tablespoons plain flour
2 tablespoons cornflour
4 tablespoons Armagnac or rum

1 Preheat the oven to warm 170°C (325°F/Gas 3). Lightly butter four deep, 9 cm (3¹/2 inch) round cake tins. Place in the refrigerator for the butter to set, then dust with flour.

2 Cream together the butter and sugar, add the baking powder and lemon rind and mix well. Add half the flour, followed by half the egg, then repeat with the remaining flour and egg, mixing well after each addition. Add the Armagnac, mix until smooth and fill a piping bag fitted with a 5 mm (1/4 inch) plain nozzle with two thirds of the mixture. Pipe a layer of the mixture onto the bottom of each of the tins, then carefully pipe about a 5 mm (1/4 inch) ring of mixture onto the sides. Smooth with a spatula and place the tins in the freezer for about 30 minutes, or until set.

3 To make the pastry cream, bring the milk to the boil in a heavy-based pan. In a bowl, whisk together the egg yolks and sugar until pale yellow in colour and the sugar has dissolved. Whisk in the flour and cornflour and mix until smooth. Once the milk has just come to the boil, pour a third into the yolk mixture to warm it before pouring in the remainder. This will prevent curdling when the yolks are mixed in with the hot milk. Pour the mixture back into the pan and blend well. Bring the mixture to the boil, stirring constantly, and cook for 1 minute. Remove from the heat and stir in the Armagnac or rum. Pour the pastry cream into a shallow dish and cover the surface with a sheet of baking paper to prevent a skin from forming. To cool quickly, place in a shallow pan of cold or iced water, changing the water until the cream is cool enough to handle. The cream can be made the day before, covered and refrigerated.

4 Once the cream has cooled, whisk vigorously until smooth. Remove the lined tins from the freezer and fill each one with some pastry cream, up to 5 mm (1/4 inch) from the top. Using the piping bag as before, pipe to cover the top of each mould with the remaining mixture and smooth the surface with a spatula dipped in water. Brush with the beaten egg, being careful not to let it drip down the edges as this will make the cakes stick and difficult to remove. Using a fork or the back of a small knife, decoratively score the tops of the cakes and bake for 30–40 minutes, or until the dough is firm and dry to the touch and is a nice golden brown. Remove from the oven and leave for 10 minutes before turning out. Cool on a wire rack. Dust with sifted icing sugar and serve.

Chef's tip Dried or canned fruit can be added to the cream for a variation, and any liqueur can be used, or the liqueur can be omitted altogether.

Chef's techniques

◆

Shaping quenelles

These oval dumplings are simmered in stock or water and used as a main meal or to garnish soups.

Bring a pan of water to the boil. Test the quenelle mixture for seasoning by cooking a teaspoon of the mixture in the simmering water.

Drain and cut through with a knife to check if it is cooked. Taste for seasoning.

Form the quenelles by scooping up some mousse with a spoon and transferring it to a second spoon, then scooping back and forth between the two spoons until the quenelle is smooth and oval with three edges.

Once formed, wet the empty spoon and use it to scoop the quenelle off the other spoon into the buttered and seasoned pan. Repeat to make about 12 quenelles.

Making Tarte Tatin

The apples give off a lot of juice, so be sure to let the sauce reduce down before adding the pastry.

Add the apples to the pan of bubbling sugar and butter and arrange upright in a circular pattern.

Make sure the apples are tightly packed as they will reduce in size as they cook. Cook and baste the apples for 45 minutes over medium heat, or until the apples are soft and the syrup has reduced and is dark brown.

Remove the apples from the heat. Working quickly, place the round of pastry on top of the apples. Use the handle of a spoon to tuck the edges into the pan.